T0380274

BIGGER DREAMS

Nana Churcher

WESTBOW
PRESS®
A DIVISION OF THOMAS NELSON
& ZONDERVAN

WestBow Press books may be ordered through booksellers or by contacting:

WestBow Press
A Division of Thomas Nelson & Zondervan
1663 Liberty Drive
Bloomington, IN 47403
www.westbowpress.com
844-714-3454

ISBN: 979-8-3850-2523-7 (sc)
ISBN: 979-8-3850-2522-0 (e)

Print information available on the last page.

WestBow Press rev. date: 07/08/2024

THIS BOOK IS WRITTEN AND DEDICATED
TO EVERYONE WHO HAS A DREAM AND
ASPIRES TO MAKE A DIFFERENCE IN LIFE.

YOU ARE THE ARTIST OF YOUR LIFE.

Contents

Chapter 1
HELLO YOU!

When God created the heaven and the earth and all that is in it, He, thought of you and I. Genesis 1 vs 1-25.

He created us in His image and likeness and blessed us. Genesis 1 vs 26-28. You were created for such a time like this, and He knew exactly who you will be. A very important person.

Jeremiah 1 vs 5
"Before I formed thee in the belly I knew thee; and before thou came forth out of the womb I sanctified thee, and I ordained thee a prophet unto the nations". You are special.

It is so important to know this truth and guard yourself from naysayers, from people who decide to label you or tarnish your image.

You are beautiful and created in God's image. Affirm this always.

Chapter 2

YOU ARE THE STAR
OF YOUR DREAM

Believe in yourself and envision your success. You've got to win in your head and with your heart before the world see you win. You are created to take dominion.

We read about the story of Joseph and his dream in the bible and how his family weren't happy about it. (Bible Reference Genesis 37 vs 5-10).

What is your dream? Magic and beautiful things happen when you dream. What do you want to do or wanted to do ever since you were a little kid? For me, it was to become a Talk Show Host, then I didn't know it was called a dream. I had this inkling that I wanted the best out of others. I wanted to tell their stories and the whole world had to hear about it.

No one believed in me, I had no journalism background, but I envisioned how the show will be like. It was going to be a Global Show. I believed in my DREAM.

Chapter 3
DARE TO DREAM

You can do anything if you dare to believe.

Jesus said to him "if you can believe, all things are possible to him who believes" Mark 9 vs 23 (NKJV)

Small dreams will suffocate you. The world belongs to those who are bold, fearless and hungry for success. Are you one of them or you are just a spectator. You have got to have a dream that others will tell you, what you are striving for is impossible.

"There are three types of people in this world: those who make things happen, those who watch things happen and those who wonder what happened." – Mary Kay Ash (Founder of Mary Kay Cosmetics)

Which of these three are you? Those who dare to dream make a difference in this world. They go against the odds and make things happen. I am very sure you have countless names, examples and stories you will want to share, how about your story.

Here are some extraordinary people who believed in the possibilities of their dream.

- The Wright brothers: Pioneers In Aeroplane
- Walt Disney: Disney World
- Sir Richard Branson: Virgin Group
- Steve Jobs: Apple lnc.
- Michael Jordan: Basketball
- Williams Sisters: Lawn Tennis
- Oprah Winfrey: Media
- Mark Zuckerberg: Facebook
- Elon Musk: SpaceX
- Pele: Football
- Muhammad Ali: Boxing
- Arnold Schwarzenegger: Actor

Chapter 4
SELF BELIEF

Whatever you have in you matters so much. The underdeveloped resources in your mind, your spirit, your inner being really counts. There is greatness in you. In each one lies that potential and ability to be developed. Dig deep and tap into the hidden treasures inside of you that needs to be harnessed. Having self-belief helps bring out the untrained abilities lying hidden in your well of greatness.

Self-belief can take your dreams and make them into blueprints. It can change the blueprint into something phenomenal. You have the ability. No one else can develop it. No one else can drive it. Believe and make it happen. I did.

The Nana Churcher Show was born, and I wrote my first book "The Power of Your Words".

Improve your self-esteem!

A. Write out a list of things you love about yourself (look yourself in the mirror and read it aloud)
B. Stop pleasing people.
C. Leave your comfort zone.
D. Let go of toxic relationships.
E. Stop comparing yourself to others.
F. Forgive yourself of past mistakes.
G. Be Positive
H. Hang out with people who will help you grow.
I. Learn something new always.
J. Celebrate your wins.

Chapter 5
BE YOUR AUTHENTIC SELF

What is mankind that you are mindful of them, human beings that you care for them? You have made them a little lower than the angels and crowned them with glory and honour. You made them rulers over the works of your hands; you put everything under their feet. (Bible reference Psalm 8 vs 4-6)

We are born to manifest the glory of God. It is not just in some of us, it is in everyone. God made you so special. There is no one like you, even twins have different traits. Each one of us is fearfully and wonderfully made.

When it comes to being authentic, one must know their worth. In a world where we are forced to compare and compete, most people have lost their sense of authenticity, they do not know their self-worth.

In a world that almost everyone wants to stand out, be an influencer or the next top model, most people have lost their sense of authenticity. A lot of people do not know what they are worth.

If you don't see yourself as a winner, then you cannot perform as a winner. You were created to take dominion. To have bigger dreams, you've got to know your worth.

What value do you place on yourself? Have you taken inventory of yourself or believed you could do something better, or you have allowed the fear of what people will say and procrastination rob you of your greatness.

Have you set a price for yourself, or anything goes? Do you have faith in yourself and the words you say?

You are worth more to yourself likely than to anyone else. Do not allow any day to go by in which you have not improved yourself. You should make yourself so valuable and authentic that men will pay a great price for you.

Set your mark, your standard high then go up there, find where your ability lies then put all your best into that ability for it to come across and put you over.

Remember you can only be the best authentic version of yourself.

VISION

When God begins to show you, your purpose and calling, there are some important steps you need to follow through. Writing things down is very important. It enables a higher level of thinking and helps for one to be focused and act. When we write we remember.

Write down the vision and make it plain on tablets that he may run who reads it. For the vision is yet for an appointed time but at the end it will speak, and it will not lie. Though it tarries, wait for it because it will surely come; it will not delay. Habakkuk 2:2-3, NIV

When you write your vision:

It allows you to submit to the power and voice of God to fulfil it.

It allows you to plan the most efficient course to your goals.

It allows you to have clarity: have a vision board with pictures of things you want to accomplish.

It allows you to detect potential setbacks before it has an impact on you.

When you have a written vision, it's not just for you. People down the line will catch you along the journey to help you fulfil it.

Chapter 7
LEAVE YOUR COMFORT ZONE, YOU WERE BORN TO WIN!

You are responsible for your life. There are many people waiting for a miracle. Yes, miracles do happen, but most of the time the one in need must take a step of faith.

Your dream comes alive when you leave your comfort zone. The place where we think we're safe can turn out to be a personal prison of our own making. Staying in your comfort zone robs you of your greatness in life. It makes you stagnant and robs you of your happiness. What are you doing to yourself? Create a position to change and add value to your life.

The greatest place on earth to find wealth is the cemetery the saying goes. There you find those who died with their dreams. Dreams that were not pursued, talents that were not developed. What are you doing with your skills, ideas, and dreams? You must have the willingness to take chances and risks, take responsibility for your life. You will experience some turbulence before you reach a higher altitude but make it happen no matter what.

In leaving your comfort zone, you must have compelling reasons to change. Do ask yourself this! WHY ARE YOU HERE?

Chapter 8
DEVELOP A WINNING ATTITUDE

Attitude is everything. It shapes your success and your happiness. Your attitude to win will propel you to your greatness. A winning attitude builds confidence. It increases your ability to take initiative and have clever ways to overcome difficulties.

Come out of your comfort zone, take risks and become the leader in your life. This is not a one-time achievement. It is a process and gradual progress of small victories. The world is your oyster.

In pursing your bigger dreams, there is nothing like an overnight success. For you to get to the top of the stairs you take it one step at a time. If you try to jump you might hurt yourself.

Whether you win or not you always gain new knowledge, skills and awareness that are only available with a winning attitude and these experiences are worth it.

Positive mindset contributes to a winning mindset. Every day we are given opportunities in life, and we must make the most out of it.

With these opportunities comes challenges, obstacles, disappointments, failures, but your mindset will determine whether to quit or thrive.

A person with a winning mindset sees him or herself-winning no matter the circumstances. If you can see yourself win, you will no matter how long, it takes.

Chapter 9
BE DISCIPLINED

Have the discipline to do little things you don't like, and you can spend your life doing the big things you do like.

You cannot build your dream without hustle. Bigger dreams start with small steps. We all have dreams but none of them can come true without self-discipline. Self-discipline begins with the mastery of your thoughts, if you don't control what you think, you can't control what you do.

Consistency is more important than the magnitude of your actions. Whatever you want to change in your life, whether it's your job, your lifestyle or being financially independent, know that steadily achieving smaller objectives onto your goal is the only way to get it. Not being hopeful.

Set small goals that are easily attained to help gain momentum, plan for the discipline you will need. For instance, if the goal is to lose weight, schedule a time to go work out at the gym and change your eating habits. Find an accountability partner who helps to keep you in check and on track. Be persistent. Working on your dream is not overnight. Be patient, but also disciplined enough to continue doing those things that will get you the result.

Chapter 10
BE CONSISTENT

Consistency comes with sacrifice. You must commit to work on your dream, come rain or shine, on good days as well as bad days. This is breathing energy into your dream. For example, if staying in shape and eating healthy is part of your goal for your dream, your working out regime must be consistent. You cannot start and stop, eat any how and expect great results.

With consistent effort, your brain gains the right neural connections due to prolonged application. It builds character and sharpens the mind. Consistent people are triumphant with unyielding inner drive. Their dedication pays off with the results that follows.

Consistency is important to help you throughout your life to find routines and methods that work for you. Once you commit to being consistent, you become regular with your routines and making plans and schedules becomes easier.

My question to you as you read is how consistent are you with the goals for your dream? Do you start and stop, or you are on it? Breathe life into your dream!

Chapter 11
BE PERSISTENT

Persistence is important, as rarely anything worth having in life comes without it. Most often, you will have to work for what you want.

Persistence gives you vital experience. When you're persistent, you learn that each failure gives you another opportunity to learn. With each failure or disappointment, you will become more resilient. You will also learn how you can overcome any challenges.

Most successful people have failed at least once but it doesn't stop them from achieving success. With each failure, they learned what they needed to do differently the next time they tried. Eventually they succeeded which would never have happened had they quit.

The saying goes "If at first you don't succeed, try again".

Persistence will motivate you to try harder. When you try and try, you will move a little closer to your goal with each attempt. This will show that your effort makes a difference. It also teaches you the value of success. Being successful takes time and effort. No one ever become successful without making sacrifices and being persistent.

Being persistent will give you the opportunity to achieve anything you set your heart on!

Chapter 12
THINK OUTSIDE
THE BOX!

It's a new year, a new month or a new day what are you doing with your life? We read in chapter 3 about dare to dream. There are those who are still thinking, dreaming and wishing to do something with their lives. Those who are waiting for the right time. In pursing your bigger dreams, one cannot play safe. You've got to take a leap of faith and think outside the box.

It is that daring spirit that makes one exceptional and people want to work with. Thinking outside the box will bring the best out of you.

Here are some traits of outside the box thinkers, let's see if you can relate.

    A. They Keep An Open Mind: Those who think outside the box are open to trying new experiences, from traveling to meeting new people and getting different perspective on life. By keeping an open mind, they allow themselves to gather more than someone who likes to follow the guidelines of 'the box'.

B. They Do Some of Their Best Thinking Alone: How do you think through the goals and plans for your bigger dreams to happen? There are those who have shared their dreams with others and were told it is impossible. But for those who think outside the box, they find a way of processing the idea they have on their own and execute. This might be going away for a retreat.

C. Passion to Make Your Bigger Dreams Happen, you must be passionate about it. Being passionate brings fresh ideas to the table. It's this passion that sustains individuals with their bigger dreams. The passion drives them even if it's painful or almost inconvenient, they will find a way.

D. They Are Learners: Life is an ongoing process. It is never finished until we depart from this planet. Until then, you must be a student for life. There is an entire world with people from all walks of life we can learn from both past and present.

E. They Seize the Moment: You must be someone who thinks outside the box to see opportunities everywhere and make the best use out of it. They look for opportunities, even in their obstacles.

Be the man or women God has created you to be, think outside the box and make your Bigger Dreams happen.

Chapter 13

THIS LITTLE LIGHT OF MINE, I AM GONNA LET IT SHINE!

You wake up one morning and all hope is lost, you want to give up, say this to yourself.

THIS LITTLE LIGHT OF MINE, I AM GONNE LET IT SHINE! You must find a way of reaching out from within to reach out to the stars. You must learn to encourage yourself and speak life to yourself.

There are many people who have given up on life and dreams, do not be counted among these people. Make your bigger dreams stay alive, persevere.

There are so many inspiring stories about people who wouldn't quit because of hard times.

One is the story of Colonel Sanders the founder of fast-food chicken KFC.

Instead of blaming others for being broke, he decided to do something with his life. He took an idea and put it into action. Many people have great ideas, but they don't put it into action. His idea was a chicken recipe. He was refused 1,009 times before he heard his first yes. Many people laughed at his face, but he persevered. How many people will keep going after 100 noes?

How many rejections and disappointment have you encountered in your bigger dreams journey? It truly takes perseverance to succeeded.

Chapter 14
MAKE DECISION!

In my local dialect (twi, an akan language in Ghana) there is a saying that goes, 'No one takes medication for the sick'. (English translation). Throughout the pages in this book, there is a power for you to change.

In building your bigger dreams and for it to happen, we must act. No one will do it for us. For us to take that action is to decide. You change when you decide and then you see progress and results.

The decisions we make have great impact on our live and determines our destiny.

Who you decide to be as a person and what you are capable of, who you decide to be with, what you decide to learn and believe, what you decide to eat or drink, all these decisions controls and directs your life. If we want change and results, then we must make new decisions and commit to it.

Chapter 15
ARE YOU READY?

Train yourself to win. Affirm yourself as a winner. Tell yourself you belong at the top. There are many people who have great ideas, dreams but aren't ready, they don't do anything about it.

Are you ready to do something about your bigger dreams, ready to be in the one percent club. Be among those who consistently work hard to make a big difference to their success.

BE PRECISE:

When you are ready to work on your bigger dreams, you must be precise on your goal. As most people start a new year by making a resolution, and the most common one is to lose weight, you should decide exactly how much you want to lose.

SET A GOAL:

Winners have great qualities that keep them at the top even though sometimes they fail.

a. Winners know their worth and are not defined by titles. They are not really a show off.

b. Winners understand success doesn't happen overnight. The behind the scenes of every successful establishment is its bed rock. Everyone who has ever built a great organization knows it takes months and years of hard work and unwavering patience and believe for great things to happen, it takes time.

c. 'Iron sharpens Iron' the saying goes. Winners spend time with other winners. They learn to build each other and share ideas. Are you ready? Hang out with eagles.

d. Your talent/gift will make room for you and bring you before great men, but you must harness it. You must train, get a coach or improve on what you've got to stand out. Are you ready to do that? That's what winners do.

e. In building your Bigger Dreams you don't dwell on your failures and blame others for it. You take responsibility of your growth. When you fail you learn from it and rise. When you own that you will continue to rise. Make your BIGGER DREAMS happen.

Chapter 16
SURROUND YOURSELF WITH GREAT PEOPLE

A story is told of an eaglet who didn't know of its greatness because it was surround by chickens. The eaglet grew with the chickens and so didn't know it could fly. The eaglet knew it was different but didn't do anything about it, till an eagle flew above it, one of its kind and it flew away.

Like the eaglet many people are hanging out with the wrong crowd. Your relationships can hold you up or down. Surround yourself with greatness, with only quality people (OQP).

Surround yourself with people who will inspire and lift you up, who will give you positive energy. Those who will help you win and give positive criticism, not those who will drain you with negative energy. What kind of friends are you hanging out with? Many have a lot of contact on their phone but are never there to help. What kind of network do you have? Is it just for parties and funerals? This is something to think about on your bigger dreams journey as many have aborted their dreams because of those they surround themselves with.

You also need to be part of a community to thrive. Seeking out and working in collaboration with others who share your interests and values will provide a stronger foundation, enabling you to reach a higher level in building your bigger dreams than you would on your own.

Chapter 17

CEASE TO BE A VICTIM

As you build your Bigger Dreams you must stop and take stock of your life. See if you are making progress, ask if you are putting maximum effort into your work.

Society has taught many to play the blame game and so whatever happens is someone's fault. Your life is an energy system. If your life is stagnant, you need to look at what you are putting in. Once you acknowledge that, your input will shape your circumstances.

The things we do to shape our circumstances are seeds. You reap what you sow after you have done the work. When you sow your seed, you work on it. You water it and wait for it to grow. The seed doesn't grow overnight. It takes time before harvest time. We live in a microwaveable world where most people want instant result without putting in the work and effort. If you want the best for your Bigger Dreams you must put in the effort.

Chapter 18
DO WHAT YOU LOVE

Doing what you love is having the passion for something and putting all your love, energy and creativity into making it work. It is taking risks and making it work and having fun doing. You have one life, spend it doing things you care about. People get paid to do what they love; they have a ball.

Many people are at a job they hate, the bills must be paid so they take on anything and get miserable, if you are in a wrong kind of job, change it. Some don't know what they want to do.

If you are one of them, maybe have you stopped listening to yourself. Many are because of hanging out with the wrong crowd or pleasing family. As you read this my question to you is do you love what you do? If the answer is yes BRAVO! And if no, rediscover your passion. Simplify your life, quit doing things out of habit, come off social media for a while, switch off the tv for thirty days, so you can see more clearly. Make time for yourself, try new things and figure it out and go from there. In building your bigger dreams, your attitude matters, it's what propels you to greatness. Love what you do and do what you love right up to the last minute.

Chapter 19
PRAY ABOUT YOUR BIGGER DREAM

Only God can make your dreams come true, so actively live for Him, and He will do the rest.

Put behind your bigger dreams only positive thoughts not negative thoughts. Pray about it to be sure it is a right objective, because if it isn't right, you will be stressed and that is not good for your health. Find a bible verse and back it with your bigger dreams.

Chapter 20
GIVE THANKS

GRATITUDE

Thank you is my favourite word. I can confidently say it's embedded in me. What about you? One of my favourite stories in the bible is Jesus and the 10 lepers (Luke 17 vs 11-19). Jesus saw and heard the lepers crying out for Him to have pity on them. He asked them to go show themselves to the priests. Out of the 10 it was only one who came back to say thank you when he realized he had been healed. A heart of gratitude. God cherishes gratitude.

Saying thank you to someone makes them feel appreciated and valued. It makes them feel happy and will make them do more for you and vice versa.

Cultivate the habit of saying thank you and keep a gratitude journal.

Wisdom Nuggets

The only person you have to face everyday is you so get your attitude right.

Be Authentic. Be You!

Have faith in God.

Believe in yourself.

Always affirm yourself positively.

Live your life. Magic happens when you are not a people pleaser.

Invest in yourself. Learn to discover your talent and harness it.

Praise and celebrate others. Celebrate life.

Don't hold people ransom and assume for others.

Be enthusiastic about what you do, have passion for your craft.

Always create an atmosphere of victory for yourself and others.

Seek godly wisdom.

If you want to be successful and prosperous meditate on the word of God and do all that it says you should do.

Always affirm you are created by God, and you are an answer.

Commit your ways to the Lord and lean not on your own understanding.

Have faith and start working on your bigger dreams!

Be kind and generous without expecting to receive from those you help.

Have an attitude of gratitude. Say thank you when your eyes open every morning, say thank you to the little things not just big stuff. Let gratitude be your lifestyle.

Be positive always.

Be mindful of your words. Words impact and have meaning.

Be prayerful.

Declutter your thoughts.

Be in charge of how you feel, master your emotions.

Free yourself from people.

Learn to change.

Learn to walk away from toxic people and environment.

Travel, explore where you live and travel the world if you can afford.

Be ambitious.

Get financial knowledge.

Read books. Read the bible and do what it says and you will make your way prosperous.

Fall in love! There is that feeling for you to experience.

Write a gratitude journal.

Be content.

Honour your word.

Don't hurt people. Try not to hurt people.

Impact lives, find a way to serve in the community.

Mentor others.

Walk away from conversations that involve hate and gossip.

Learn to shut your mouth, less talk and do more.

Your commitment to yourself has to come from your heart not your head.

Grow your mindset.

Spend time with people you love.

Exercise daily.

Don't start a relationship If you are not in love.

Don't care about what people think.

Take more risks.

Make a list of things you want to have happen.

Take stock of your life and be responsible.

Don't chase, attract .

God bless and know that **"You Belong At The TOP"**.

Printed in the United States
by Baker & Taylor Publisher Services